Contents

Welcome to Brazil

Brazil is the largest country in South America. It is almost the same size as the USA. Brazil is famous for huge forests, colourful carnivals and a world-beating football team.

On the east, its 8,000-kilometre-long Atlantic Ocean coastline has landscapes ranging from golden beaches to wild swamps. The River Amazon crosses Brazil at the equator from west to east. To the north, west and south, Brazil borders with ten other South American countries.

Brazilians have their origins in many races. Almost 500 years ago, Portuguese settlers arrived from Europe and intermarried with the Native Americans. Many years later, other people landed from such places such as Italy, the Netherlands, West Africa and Japan. Today, most Brazilians speak Portuguese and they are creating one of the world's most vibrant and multicultural nations.

Brazil is a young person's country. Music is everywhere; cinema, books and magazines abound. Televison has an enormous audience and reaches even distant parts of the Amazon forests.

DATABASE

For reasons of climate, migration and work, Brazil has distinct peoples and cultures in different regions. For example, the coastal region south of the equator has a strong West African culture, while further south tends to be European. The great interior is simply 'Brazilian', although there are now very few Native Americans living there.

Brazilians and tourists alike relax on Copacabana beach and swim in the Atlantic Ocean at Rio de Janeiro. ▼

Country File
Brazil

Marion Morrison

FRANKLIN WATTS
LONDON • SYDNEY

First published in 2003 by
Franklin Watts
96 Leonard Street, London
EC2A 4XD

Franklin Watts Australia
45–51 Huntley Street,
Alexandria, NSW 2015

COUNTRY FILE: BRAZIL produced for Franklin Watts by
Bender Richardson White, PO Box 266, Uxbridge, UK.
Editor: Lionel Bender
Designer and Page Make-up: Ben White
Picture Researcher: Cathy Stastny
Cover Make-up: Mike Pilley, Radius
Production: Kim Richardson

Graphics and Maps: Stefan Chabluk

Consultant: Dr Terry Jennings, a former geography teacher
and university lecturer. He is now a full-time writer of
children's geography and science books.

A CIP catalogue record for this book is available
from the British Library.

ISBN 0-7496-4816-3

Manufactured in China

Picture Credits

Pages: 1: PhotoDisc Inc./Ernesto Rios Lanz/Sexto Sol.
3: PhotoDisc Inc./Adalberto Rios Lanz/Sexto Sol. 4: James
Davis Travel Photography. 7: PhotoDisc Inc./Glen Allison.
8: South American Pictures/Tony Morrison. 10: South
American Pictures/Tony Morrison. 11: James Davis Travel
Photography. 12: South American Pictures/Tony
Morrison. 13: South American Pictures/Tony Morrison.
14: South American Pictures/Tony Morrison. 15: South
American Pictures/Tony Morrison. 17: South American
Pictures/Tony Morrison. 18: James Davis Travel
Photography. 19: South American Pictures/Tony
Morrison. 20: James Davis Travel Photography.
21: South American Pictures/Jason P. Howe. 22: South
American Pictures/Jason P. Howe. 23: Eye
Ubiquitous/Robert Donaldson. 24: Eye Ubiquitous/
J. Waterlow. 26: South American Pictures/Tony Morrison.
29: South American Pictures/Index Editoria.
30: PhotoDisc Inc./Adalberto Rios Lanz/Sexto Sol
31: PhotoDisc Inc./Colin Paterson.
Cover photo: James Davis Travel Photography.

The Author

Marion Morrison is a writer and editor
of books on the countries of South
America. With her photographer
husband, Tony Morrison, she runs the
photo library *South American Pictures*.

70°W   60°W   50°W   40°W

10°N

VENEZUELA

GUYANA

COLOMBIA

SURINAME **FRENCH GUIANA**

ATLANTIC

OCEAN

N
W   E
S

Boa Vista

Amapá

Macapá

△ Pico da Neblina

Branco

Negro

Belém

São Luis

0°

Japurá

Manaus

Santarém

A m a z o n

Fortaleza

Fernando de Noronha

Atol das Rocas

Solimões

Tocantins

Teresina

Marabá

Xingu

Tapajós

Madeira

Juruá

Purus

Porto Velho

PERU

Rio Branco

Parnaíba

Recife

São Francisco

Maceió

10°S

Juazeiro

Barragem de Sobradinho

Salvador

B R A Z I L

MINAS GERAIS

P L A N A L T O   D E

Culabá

□ BRASILIA

M A T O   G R O S S O

Montes Claros

BOLIVIA

Campo Grande

São José do Rio Preto

SERRA DA CANASTRA

Belo Horizonte

Paraná

20°S

PARAGUAY

São Paulo

Rio de Janeiro

Itaipú

Santos

Iguaçu Falls

Tropic of Cancer

Curitiba

ATLANTIC

CHILE

*S
E
R
R
A
D
O
M
A
R*

OCEAN

PACIFIC OCEAN

Uruguay

30°S

Pôrto Alegre

ARGENTINA

URUGUAY

	Mountains	△ Mountain peak
	Grassland and farming	
□	Capital	○ Major city
	Country boundary	

0   1000 Miles

0   1000 Kilometres

The Land

At the widest point, Brazil stretches 4,330 kilometres from east to west. From north to south in Brazil, the longest distance is 4,320 kilometres. The highest point is at 3,014 metres on *Pico da Neblina*, the forested 'Peak of Mists' in the northern state of Amazonas.

In such a large country, nowhere can be thought of as average. Parts of the north-east are so dry that in some years people have to migrate to find water. In contrast, some parts of the southern coast suffer from floods every year. Often there is frost in the south and occasionally it snows. Landslides due to summer rain are frequent on the hills surrounding the beautiful coastal city of Rio de Janeiro.

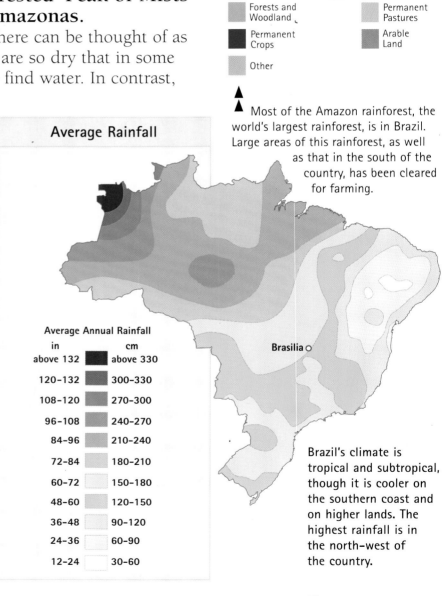

1% 5% 22% 14% 58%

- Forests and Woodland
- Permanent Crops
- Other
- Permanent Pastures
- Arable Land

▲ Most of the Amazon rainforest, the world's largest rainforest, is in Brazil. Large areas of this rainforest, as well as that in the south of the country, has been cleared for farming.

Average Rainfall

Average Annual Rainfall	
in	cm
above 132	above 330
120–132	300–330
108–120	270–300
96–108	240–270
84–96	210–240
72–84	180–210
60–72	150–180
48–60	120–150
36–48	90–120
24–36	60–90
12–24	30–60

Brasilia ○

Brazil's climate is tropical and subtropical, though it is cooler on the southern coast and on higher lands. The highest rainfall is in the north-west of the country.

Time Zones

Brazil has three time zones, each one hour apart. The easternmost zone is 3 hours behind Greenwich Mean Time, so when it is 6.00 a.m. in London, it is 3.00 a.m. in Rio de Janeiro. The clocks on Fernando de Noronha, a group of 19 small islands 345 kilometres from the coast, are one hour ahead of Rio – it will be 4.00 a.m.

 The Iguaçu Falls form part of the border between Brazil and Argentina. This section is known as the Deodoro Falls. The River Iguaçu is a tributary of the River Paraná.

Animals

The Amazon rainforest contains a greater number of plant species than any other habitat on earth and Brazil's forests contain thousands of different species of plants and animals. The largest mammal is the tapir, a pig-like animal but a relative of the horse. It can weigh up to 250 kilograms. The smallest mammals are rodents that weigh as little as 20 grams.

One Amazon catfish, the *piraiba*, can weigh more than 200 kilograms. A parrot of the north-east, Spixs' macaw, is the rarest bird in the world. It inhabits the dry scrub grasslands known as the *caatinga*, but is believed to have become extinct in the wild in July 2002.

Rivers and landscape

Almost half of Brazil is dominated by the River Amazon. It has thousands of tributary rivers, although not all begin within the country's boundaries. Also, not all the banks of the Amazon are forested. Some are swampy, while other banks are grasslands or dry scrub.

In south-west Brazil, the River Paraná is also a giant. It gathers water from 11 per cent of the country then flows south to the sea through Argentina. Rainfall in this region of Brazil is so heavy that dams on the Paraná are able to generate enormous hydro-electric power.

The only major river that is totally Brazilian is the 3,161-kilometre-long São Francisco. It rises in the Serra da Canastra north-west of Rio de Janeiro and flows northwards through a region that in places is almost a desert. The river is used for irrigating farmland.

Web Search ►►

► http://www.ibge.
gov.br
A huge database of information about the country, from the Brazilian Institute of Geography and Statistics; there is an option to read the information in English.

The People

The population of Brazil is increasing by approximately 3 million people each year. By the end of 2002 the population was estimated at 175,572,385. About half the people are less than 25 years old.

Most Brazilians are descended from European ancestry and some of the immigrant communities still retain their own identity. Swiss-Germans settled in forested mountains to the north-east of Rio de Janeiro in 1819. Germans began to arrive in 1824 and headed to the cooler south. The main German towns are in the southern states of Rio Grande do Sul and Santa Catarina.

Arabs, Lebanese and Syrians arrived between 1860 and 1890 and worked in the rubber trade in the Amazon region where today many shops have names of Middle Eastern origin. Japanese immigrants first settled in São Paulo in 1908 and started to cultivate land. Later some Japanese moved into other jobs and now they are the most prosperous of all the ethnic groups.

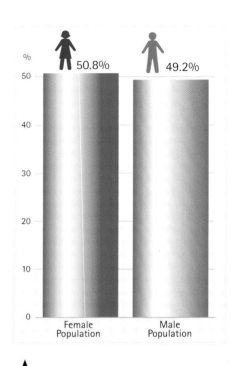

▲ The proportion of males and females in the Brazilian population.

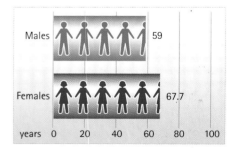

▲ A comparison of the average life expectancy of males and females in Brazil.

◄◄ Mestiço street vendors selling food in the coastal town of Salvador.

8

Population

The population of Brazil is concentrated in the south and along the coast, away from the dense northern rainforests.

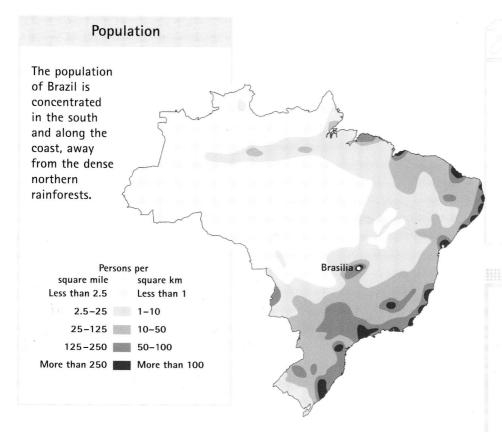

Persons per

square mile	square km
Less than 2.5	Less than 1
2.5–25	1–10
25–125	10–50
125–250	50–100
More than 250	More than 100

Brasilia

Language

Brazilians speak Portuguese but with some differences from the language of Portugal. For example, *taxi* stands for a taxicab but in Brazil it is also the word used in the north-east for an ant tree or the ants living in the stalks of the tree's leaves.

DATABASE

Japanese generations

The Japanese of São Paulo keep their traditional name for each generation or *sei*. First generation immigrants were the *issei*. Second generation are the *nissei*. Third generation are *sansei*. Fourth generation are *yonsei*.

 Web Search ►►

► http://www.funai. gov.br
National Indian Foundation/ Fundação Nacional do Indio has information about the Native Americans in Portuguese.

► http://www.ibge. gov.br
The Brazilian Institute of Geography and Statistics website has a 'population clock' updated monthly.

aThe Native Americans and *mestiçoes*

In the early sixteenth century, explorers called the country 'The Land of Brazil' after a wood found there that had the colour of glowing embers, or *brasa* in Portuguese. At that time, there are thought to have been well over two million Native Americans. Today, only some 100,000 survive. Many have kept their original languages but Portuguese is spoken widely. A few tribal groups in the heart of the forest still have no contact with the modern Brazilians and are known to exist just by signs left at the edge of their territory.

Close to 40 per cent of Brazilians are *mestiço* or people of mixed racial origin. Of these, by far the largest proportion are the *mulattos* of mixed black African races and Portuguese. Others are descendants of Native Americans and Africans, and Native Americans and Europeans. All are bound together by the special national bond of beliefs, traditions and customs that unites Brazilians.

Urban and Rural Life

More than 80 per cent of Brazilians live in towns and cities. São Paulo is the largest city and home to almost 20 million people. It is second only to Mexico City as the largest metropolitan area in the world.

Brasilia, the capital of Brazil, has two million people. In contrast, much of the Amazon basin has less than one person per square kilometre.

In modern Brazil, the energy of the *Paulistas* – the people of São Paulo state – is legendary. Their skill in banking and industry has created the economic powerhouse of Brazil and South America as a whole. São Paulo was founded by the Portuguese in 1554 and it was from there that organized expeditions set out into the interior. The expeditioners were known as *bandeirantes* because each group had its own *bandeira*, or flag. Some of the groups numbered up to 3,000 men. The going was tough, but they claimed vast tracts of land. The Portuguese explorers settled in small numbers to farm the interior.

DATABASE

Housing

For some people life in the cities of Brazil means fine houses or apartments but for many it is simple shanties or *favelas*. In the country, people live in housing ranging from grand *fazendas* or estates to palm-roofed shelters in the forest. Brasilia, the capital, was planned with living units of apartments and nearby shops and entertainment such as clubs and cinemas. 'Satellite' towns now surround Brasilia. Some people live or work in these while others commute to often low-paid jobs in the city.

Buses and cars fill the streets of the financial centre in São Paulo.

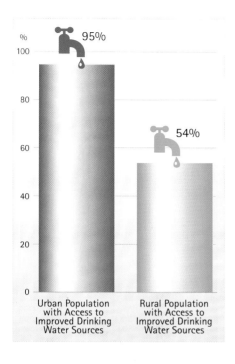

◄◄ A comparison of the percentage of people with access to improved drinking water sources.

In the Amazon rainforest, many families live in houses made of timber, thatch and palm leaves. ▼
▼

Drinking Water

While most Brazilians can obtain clean drinking water, few have running water in their homes. Both urban and rural dwellers have to queue at a standpipe – a main outlet on the street – to get drinking water. In north-east Brazil in particular, some people queue for hours for water.

Population movements

In the late-1500s, when natural riches were discovered in the north and along the coast, great migrations to these regions followed. In the seventeenth century, diamonds and gold attracted people into Minas Gerais. Wild rubber from forest trees drew thousands of migrants to the Amazon region in the late-nineteenth century. The construction of the new capital, Brasilia, led tens of thousands more – the *candangos* – into the middle of the country in the late 1950s.

Amazonian development

A Trans-Amazon Highway project of the 1970s spurred settlement in Amazonia. A gold rush to eastern Amazonia south of Macapá occurred in the 1980s. By the end of the twentieth century, the map of Brazil had changed. Fine asphalt-covered roads led to almost every corner, and modern airlines delivered passengers in wide-bodied jets across the country. Today, Manaus, the Amazon regional capital, has 1.5 million inhabitants and is a thriving city.

Web Search ►►

► http://www1.ibge.gov.
br/brasil_em_sintese/
default.htm
A Brazilian government site showing a map of population density. Go to 'Fazer download do mapa grande' to download the large map.

Farming and Fishing

Less than 50 years ago, Brazil was known for just one crop, coffee. Almost half of the world's coffee production came from there. In recent years, Brazil has developed huge agribusinesses that now account for 21 per cent of Gross Domestic Product.

The densely populated south-east is the centre for the cultivation of coffee and soya beans. Orange juice from São Paulo state is exported worldwide. Brazil has five tanker ships that are dedicated to carrying the frozen juice to the USA and northern Europe. Land along the coast has been cultivated for generations, and sugar cane is farmed extensively in the north-east. Fishing, for local consumption, is important. Large quantities of fish are caught along the coast and in the rivers.

Irrigation schemes

Major irrigation schemes have brought more land under cultivation. Dry land round the Rio São Francisco now produces melons, grapes and oranges for export. The fruits are transported in specially chilled shipping containers that are taken 500 kilometres by road to the coast. The huge strides in agricultural production make it appear that Brazil is simply a giant farm, but that is not the case.

Fishing

As Amazon cities and towns have grown, so has the demand for fish until some species are becoming scarce. One of the largest freshwater fish is the pirarucu. It can weigh 140 kilograms but most of those caught are about 30 kilograms, and even that size is declining around markets such as Manaus and Belém. Along the coast fishermen work with many types of small boats and the catches include shrimps, crabs, lobsters, corvina, swordfish and shark. Most shellfish are sold in local markets but some are exported.

Mechanized farming in São Paulo state. Here, maize is being cut to make silage, a food for farm animals. ▼

▲▲ Cattle ranching is a major industry in the central and southern plateau regions. Cowboys in the south of the country are known as *gauchos*.

Local production

Small-scale farmers still work for the local markets. Some have a hectare or less of land and barely make a living from growing fruit or root crops.

In the rural areas, most homes have space for growing only their own root crops. The majority of Native Americans have their 'gardens' for growing age-old natural crops such as mandioca (manioc or cassava). Native Americans also catch fish in the rivers. Baited hooks and nylon lines are replacing the old methods of bow and arrow and fish traps.

Farming

The south and coastal region are the main agricultural areas.

Brasilia

- 🐂 Cattle
- 🐖 Pigs
- 🐑 Sheep
- 🍊 Citrus Fruit
- ☕ Coffee
- 🌱 Cotton
- Soya Beans
- Sugar Cane
- 🌳 Timber

Pasture

Cropland

Forest

Web Search ►►

► http://www.ibge. gov.br

The Brazilian Statistics Institute site has farming and fishing statistics that are updated every 3 months. There is also news about the problems faced by Brazilian farmers and fishermen.

Resources and Industry

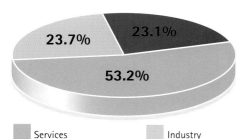

23.1%
23.7%
53.2%

Services
Industry
Agriculture

▲ Proportion of the workforce in the three main areas of employment in Brazil.

At Carajás open-cast mine, huge mechanical shovels are used to gather iron ore for export or for processing in foundries within Brazil. ▼

During the twentieth century, Brazil changed from a purely agricultural producer to an industrialized nation in a series of leaps. One of the greatest leaps was during the 1970s when, by using loans from abroad, industry took off dramatically.

Much of the development has brought changes to the environment. In 1986 production at the enormous Carajás iron deposits in eastern Amazonia began, and a railway 890 kilometres long was built to carry the ore to the coast. To make way for this, large areas of rainforest were destroyed and increased mining polluted many rivers.

São Paulo expanded to become an industrial heartland. In its factories today, vehicles are produced for home use and export. The country has its own aircraft industry and exports small passenger planes. The supermarkets are filled with goods 'Made in Brazil'.

The Environment

Brazil holds the key to the greatest rainforest reserves in the world. Environmentalists believe that expansion into the Amazon basin will destroy the forest, so protective measures have been taken. Large national parks and forest reserves have been established and elsewhere there are some controls on the way the forest is used. Schemes to replant trees felled for timber are actively promoted.

Energy

Brazil has its own oil reserves that are mainly offshore to the south-east of Rio de Janeiro. Energy also comes from coal, gas and hydropower. One of the world's largest hydro-electric plants, Itaipú, was completed on the River Paraná in 1985. Gas for the energy-hungry São Paulo region is imported from neighbouring Bolivia along a 3,150-kilometre-long pipeline opened in 2001.

Encouraging industry

One of the most enterprising of all the economic ideas of the 1950s was the creation of a 'free trade zone' around Manaus in Amazonia. Special tax laws apply there and many companies, especially in electronics, have set up factories. Goods made in Manaus are then exported to the rest of Brazil, South America and places worldwide. Many of the workers are women, and each day specially hired buses take them from their homes to the factories.

A car factory assembly line. Many of the cars built in Brazil are exported around the world. ▼

Resources and Industry

- Car Manufacture
- Chemicals
- Electronics
- $ Finance
- Food Processing
- Iron and Steel
- Mining
- Oil
- Printing and Publishing
- Textiles
- Timber Processing
- Tourism
- Hydro-electricity

○ Brasilia

Most of Brazil's natural resources lie in the Amazon region and offshore; its factories are centred on cities in the east of the country.

🌐 **Web Search** ▶▶

▶ http://www.suframa.gov.br
To learn more about the extraordinary 'Zona Franca' in the middle of the Amazon rainforest, try the official site.

▶ http://www.embratur.gov.br
This site set up by the Brazilian Tourist Office has a good 'Children's Corner'.

Transport

For a country the size of Brazil, a good transport system is essential. For the first European settlers, the interior was almost inaccessible. They used the rivers, particularly in Amazonia, until trails were cut through the forests.

The first railway line was built in 1852 and was soon followed by lines reaching inland from the coast. Then proper roads were built and these were improved during the 1970s and '80s with super-highways, some of them thousands of kilometres long.

Bus travel

Long-distance travel is mostly by buses. At the top end of the market is the *Expresso luxo* or luxury express. These buses have air-conditioning, sleeper seats and television. At the cheaper end most services are comfortable and reliable. Virtually every town has an *estação rodoviária* or bus station. The best have monitor screens with timetables, booking offices, showers, restaurants and shops. A journey from Brasilia to Belém at the mouth of the Amazon may take two days. Seat-numbered tickets are bought in advance, luggage is checked in and the bus stops at most towns along the way.

Cars and underground railways

Cars – even old ones – are a luxury and are owned only by well-paid office, factory or professional Brazilians. Everyone else uses the local buses or taxis. Rio de Janeiro and São Paulo have modern, efficient metro systems. Curitiba – a city in the south – prides itself on its 'green' transport. Buses use special routes and have small, covered passenger stations on the pavement where tickets are bought before boarding.

Air transport

Wealthy Brazilians, or those who have borrowed from friends and family, usually choose to fly the long distances within the country. Brazilian airlines have modern jets and major airports are of a high standard. Hundreds of minor towns and settlements have smaller airports that are often no more than a hut beside an earth runway. They are served by regional airlines using propeller aircraft carrying a dozen passengers or less.

Ways to travel

Some curiosities of early transport have survived. Part of the Rio de Janeiro tramway system runs between the old city centre and the hillside suburb of Santa Teresa. In Salvador, which is built on a hill, the upper and lower parts of the town are connected by a funicular railway – two steeply inclined tracks carrying cabins which are hauled up or down by cables.

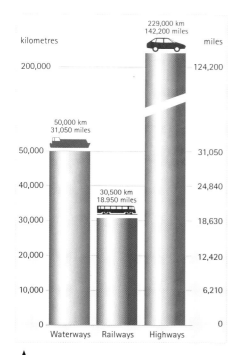

A comparison of the lengths of the main transport systems.

▲ Many cars run on alcohol that is derived from sugar cane.

Transport

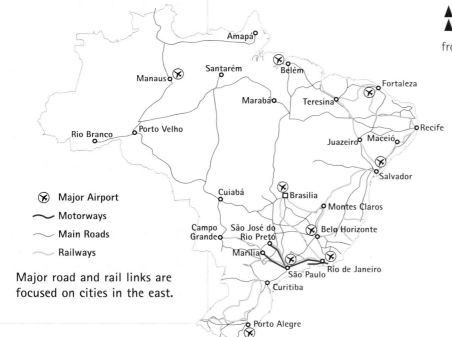

(x) Major Airport

〜 Motorways

〜 Main Roads

〜 Railways

Major road and rail links are focused on cities in the east.

🌐 **Web Search** ▶▶

▶ http://www.varig.com.
br/english/index.htm
The site of Varig, the Brazilian national airline.

▶ http://www.mp.usp.
br.mamore.htm
From the Museum of São Paulo, this shows the 'Devil's Railway' of the 1800s that survives in parts of the Amazon forest.

Education

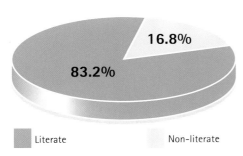

16.8%

83.2%

Literate   Non-literate

▲ The percentages of people in Brazil who are able or unable to read and write.

Approximately one in five Brazilians are of school age. Once they are 7 years old, most children attend school until they are 14. Some continue in secondary school until they are 18. A few do not attend school at all, and about 20 per cent of the population cannot read or write.

The state provides many schools while others are run by the church. Especially in the cities, schools may be private, with families paying fees. At secondary level, classroom space is often limited and students attend in shifts. This system helps the school and also gives the students time to work to earn money.

At the age of 18, pupils take an exam to qualify for university or college entrance. There are many universities. University graduates may go directly to work in Brazil. The lucky few will find scholarships to attend further courses or do research in other countries. Brazil creates fine surgeons, scientists, and other professionals.

A village school built on the banks of a river in Amazonia. The building is raised off the ground to avoid flood damage. ▼

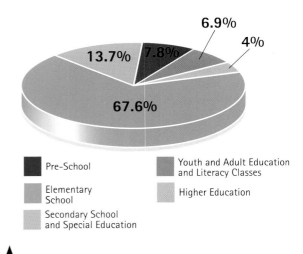

6.9%

4%

13.7% 7.8%

67.6%

Pre-School   Youth and Adult Education and Literacy Classes

Elementary School   Higher Education

Secondary School and Special Education

▲ Proportions of pupils and students in the various educational establishments in Brazil.

Universities

At university level, many students have to leave home to study at distant universities. Some live with local families. Many parents work extra hours to ensure that their children get a better education than was possible when they were young.
At every level of education, the environment is a national issue. Non-government organizations raise money from business or selling T-shirts and books to fund their educational programmes.

▲ Pupils in a classroom in a primary state school in Caerá, north-east Brazil.

Providing for an education

In rural communities, classes begin early in the day and finish at midday. This gives children time to help their parents work on the land or at their crafts. Even small villages have two or sometimes three schools to which the children walk or travel by public bus.

Cities have schools in each area, and most state pupils walk to school. Schools in towns and cities have the advantage that Brazil is well equipped with museums and places that hold exhibitions. Some pupils have the chance to visit these educational centres as part of their studies.

Radio, television and the internet now carry education to many more people. The Brazilian government, institutions and many companies have children's, or 'teens', pages on their internet sites. Some newspapers and magazines are extremely aware of their responsibilities and have well-illustrated educational sections.

 Web Search ►►

► http://www.inep.gov.br/idiomas/ingles.htm
This site includes downloadable files of the National Education Plan and exam samples.

► http://www.stpauls.br/
A long-established private school in São Paulo – the site is in English and has pictures of the school.

► http://www.unb.br/
The showcase university of the capital city, opened in the 1960s.

► http://www.inpa.gov.br
The National Amazon Research Institute site is in Portuguese and has an English version 'under construction'.

Sport and Leisure

Football

Brazil has 35 major football clubs. Rio de Janeiro has the famous Maracana Stadium, with seating for 125,000 and standing for 30,000. It may have slipped in world size ranking to third but it still holds the record for the 199,854 spectators who watched the World Cup final in 1950. Brazil has won the World Cup five times. 'Pele' is Brazil's most famous football star. In his career he played 1,362 games, scoring an incredible 1,280 goals.

Above all other sports, Brazilians are dedicated to football. Go into a Brazilian street on the day of a big football match and it will be empty while everyone is glued to the television. Go into the same street if the home team loses and it will be filled with gloom.

Motor racing is a close second in popularity followed by volleyball, tennis, basketball, swimming and cycling. Many younger Brazilians with some money to spend are involved with outdoor activities such as trekking, climbing and sailing.

The Brazilian Olympic team won 12 medals in the 2000 games in Sydney, Australia. Brazilian athletes also compete in the PanAmerican games held every four years. Most large towns have special facilities for disabled athletes, and the country sends teams to compete in world paraplegic events. Sixty-four wheelchair athletes went to the Sydney Paralympic Games in 2000 and they gained 22 medals.

Playing volleyball on the beach at Rio de Janeiro. In the background is Sugar Loaf Mountain (shown on the cover of this book). ▼

DATABASE

Leisure Time

Chess is played in homes, in community halls, in the parks and by the beach. Brazil has an annual chess championship and competes internationally.
For the more active, there are hiking groups and groups for kayaking, paragliding and microlight flying. Climbing is restricted to places with cliffs or big rocks such as those around Rio de Janeiro. Horse-riding is popular in both urban and rural areas.

▲
The Maracana football stadium in Rio de Janeiro, the third largest in the world.

Motor racing

Rio de Janeiro and São Paulo have internationally famous motor racing tracks – the Jacarepaguá and Interlagos respectively. They take it in turn to hold the Formula One Brazilian Grand Prix.

Three Brazilian drivers – Emerson Fittipaldi, Nelson Piquet and Ayrton Senna – dominated the Formula One events for 30 years. Fittipaldi was winner of the Driver's Championship twice in the 1970s, Piquet won it three times in the '80s, and Senna was the star of the 1990s. He won the Driver's Championship three times. When Senna died in a motor racing accident in Italy in 1994, the entire country was in mourning for days.

Web Search ▶▶

▶ http://www.futbrasil.
com/arquivo/rankings/
placar.html
A list of the Brazilian football clubs and their rankings.

▶ http://www.360soccer.
com/pele
Read about the career of Pele – Edson Arantes do Nasciemento – the world's greatest footballer.

▶ http://www.senna.
globo.com/instituto
ayrtonsenna
This organization, set up by Ayrton Senna, helps young people across Brazil ; the site is only in Portuguese.

Daily Life and Religion

On Easter Day 1500, Portuguese explorers landed on the Atlantic coast of South America near a hill they named *Monte Pascoal* or Easter Hill. The country they named *Santa Cruz* or Good Cross, but that was soon changed to Brazil.

The explorers brought with them the Catholic religion, and today small wayside chapels are still known by the old name of *Santa-Cruz*. The Native Americans whom the explorers encountered had their own simple religion based on forest spirits, the earth and sky. The Europeans soon converted them to Catholicism. Then came the black African slaves with their own religion, some of which has survived. Immigrants brought other faiths to the country.

Today in Brazil, evangelical churches – especially from North America – are having a profound effect in some cities. In São Paulo, where life is pressured for many and without hope for many more, the evangelical churches are followed by millions of people. Radio is important for spreading the teaching of these churches.

A papier mâché figure of Judas Iscariot is carried through the streets during a Holy Week parade. ▼

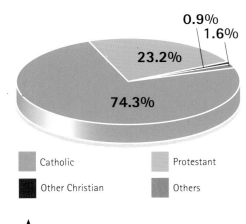

0.9%
1.6%
23.2%
74.3%

- ■ Catholic
- ■ Protestant
- ■ Other Christian
- ■ Others

▲ Followers of the major faiths in Brazil. Most Brazilians are Catholic, as are the majority of South Americans.

▲
For the Carnival in Rio De Janeiro, performers appear in stunning costumes.

The working week

Brazilians do not all work the same hours. Many shops in the south-east may not open until 9 or even 10 a.m. but they close late in the day. In the heat of Amazonia, some shops close at midday and then stay open until 10 p.m. Local markets begin soon after dawn. Offices often open early and close when the work is finished. Traffic in São Paulo is moving all night and the first commuter flight for Rio de Janeiro leaves before 7 a.m. Sundays are for leisure.

Health care

Free health care is available to every Brazilian, paid for by the tax system. Towns and cities have hospitals, and in rural areas there is usually a medical post. A national vaccination programme exists for young children. Brazil produces large quantities of pharmaceuticals for home and export markets. Many wealthy Brazilians pay for private treatment through healthcare schemes.

Carnival

Carnival (*Carnaval* in Portuguese) is a time of great happiness and enjoyment for Brazilians. It is held over the weekend before Ash Wednesday, the beginning of the Christian period of Lent, but the modern festival seems to have little connection with religion.

Web Search ►►

► http://www.nova
jerusalem.com.br
Looks at The Suffering of Christ Easter passion play at Nova Jerusalem in north-east Brazil.

► http://www.brasilia
convention.com.br/
english/default.asp
Site of the Brasilia Convention Centre, which has shops, cinemas, theatres and exhibitions.

Arts and Media

Brazil is a media country where television draws massive audiences. Satellites beam channels to every region. Music is full of rhythm and very 'Brazilian' – noisy, lively and melodic. It is followed by a wide audience outside the country. Live concerts fill arenas, beaches and theatres.

Away from the intensely youthful modern Brazil there is a strong cultural tradition supported by world famous writers, composers, musicians and movie-makers.

The Brazilian media giant, *Globo*, runs a leading newspaper and the country's most successful television channel, *Rede Globo* or Globo Network. The channel owns 113 transmitters covering 99.85 per cent of the 5,443 municipalities, or local areas, in Brazil. Some television programmes have audiences of over 120 million.

Editora Abril in São Paulo is a huge publishing house of books and magazines. One of its best known magazines, *Veja*, has a circulation of 1.2 million, and delivery trucks drive 150,000 kilometres a week to distribute it.

Writers

Some Brazilian writers are international names. Jorge Amado from Salvador wrote 30 novels, many using themes from the deep-rooted Afro-Brazilian culture of the north-east. Gilberto Freyre wrote classics about Brazilian social history, especially the sugar plantation era in the eighteenth and nineteenth centuries.

Music

Brazilian dance music is known around the world and the beat of the *samba* is the sound of Carnival. It has its roots in African culture. The north-east of Brazil produces many of the country's best singers. Perhaps the best known piece of Brazilian classical music is *Bachianas Brasileiras* by the renowned composer Heitor Villa Lobos.

◄◄ The Opera House in Manaus.

24

Newspapers and magazines

The media cover the country. For example, Rio Branco on an Amazon tributary is 2,700 kilometres from São Paulo and has a population of 253,000. Today it is best known for the time in 1988 when Chico Mendes, a forest rubber tapper trying to save the environment, was assassinated by land developers in a nearby town. Rio Branco has its own paper, *O Rio Branco*, and a local TV station. The newspaper and the TV schedules can be found on line. Air services deliver other newspapers and magazines from the south-east.

Famous films

The list of Brazilian film names begins with the vivacious Carmen Miranda, who swept to fame in the 1930s and 1940s with 19 films. More recently a young director from Rio de Janeiro, Walter Salles, has won international prizes for his work such as *Central Station* and *Behind the Sun*, both set in the north-east of Brazil.

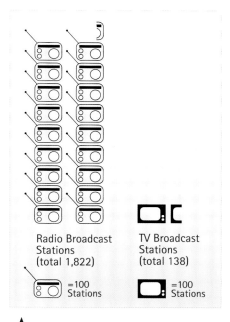

Radio Broadcast Stations (total 1,822)

TV Broadcast Stations (total 138)

= 100 Stations

= 100 Stations

▲ Brazil has a vast number of local radio stations and TV broadcasters.

Growth in number of foreign tourists visiting Brazil. ▼

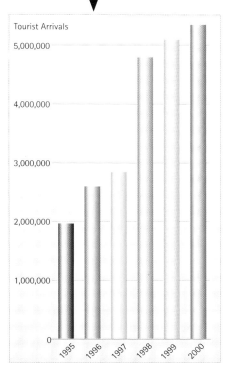

Tourist Arrivals

5,000,000

4,000,000

3,000,000

2,000,000

1,000,000

0

1995 1996 1997 1998 1999 2000

DATABASE

Tourism

Embratur, the official Brazilian tourism organization, has for many years promoted the country as a tourist paradise, and world interest is growing, especially for wilderness trips. In the far west of the country, the Pantanal – a huge swamp rich with wildlife – is a popular destination. Brazilian beaches are another magnet and particularly in the south there are resort developments attracting visitors from Argentina and Uruguay.

Web Search ►►

► http://www.lyngsat.com/ brasilb1.shtml
See the channels and areas covered by a satellite parked in orbit above Brazil.

► http://www.uol.com.br/ criancas/vejakid.htm
Site of the children's version of the magazine Veja *in Portuguese*

► http://www.uol.com.br/ allbrazilianmusic
All Brazilian Music, *the music from Brazil (in English).*

Government

Brazil is a democratic republic – its full name is the Federative Republic of Brazil. There are 26 states, and 1 federal district that surrounds Brasilia, the capital. Each state has a governor and its own administration.

Each state sends elected representatives to the National Congress in Brasilia. The president is the head of state and the government, and leads the country from the capital. The presidential palace is the *Planalto Palace* and the presidential house is separate from this.

Brazil declared independence from Portugal on 7 September 1822 and has passed through some difficult times to reach its present constitution with an elected government. Most recently, Brazil was ruled by the military from 1964 to 1985, when elections were resumed. All Brazilians between the ages of 18 and 70 must vote. Presidential elections are held every four years and the president may run for a second term.

Brasilia

At the beginning of the nineteenth century, Rio de Janeiro was the capital of Brazil. In 1955 Juscelino Kubitschek, a presidential candidate of immense vision, promised to move the capital to a new site in the interior. The chosen location was at an altitude of 1,360 metres on the *Planalto* or high plain of Goias, roughly in the centre of the country. Kubitschek became president in 1956 and construction began in the same year, even before approval of the final plan. Kubitschek inaugurated the new capital, Brasilia, on 21 April 1960.

The Palace of Congress in Brasilia. ▼

Congress

The National Congress consists of a federal senate of 81 seats made up of elected members from each state and the federal district. The Chamber of Deputies, also elected from the individual states, has 513 members. The president appoints the cabinet that controls the nation's affairs, including economic, foreign, health and educational policies. Government departments and institutions implement the policies and make suggestions for changes.

Justice

The highest court in Brazil is the Supreme Federal Tribunal of 11 ministers appointed by the president and confirmed by the senate. Below this there is a Supreme Tribunal of Justice responsible for the ordinary laws. Regional federal tribunals are composed of at least seven judges, usually from the local area. There are special military tribunals for cases of crime in the armed forces.

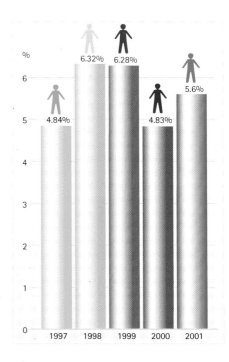

In recent years, about 1 in 20 of the workforce has been unemployed.

Regions and States

Administratively, Brazil is divided up into regions, then states and the federal district of Brasilia, and finally into municipal areas.

Web Search ▶▶

▶ http://www.infobrasilia.com.br/bsb_hi.htm
The history of Brasilia – the English version with photographs.

▶ http://brasil.gov.br
Official access site to the departments of the Government of Brazil.

▶ http://www.planalto.gov.br
Site of the Presidential Office, with a biography of the president and a picture tour of the palace and its art collection (in Portuguese).

Place in the World

Brazil is known for its music, football and carnival. Beyond that popular image it has an even stronger place in the world as the largest South American nation, the world's eighth largest economy, and a partner in *Mercosur* – a regional trading organization that is the world's fourth largest economic market.

Brazil hosted the great world environmental conference in 1992 – the Earth Summit – and has signed all the major environmental agreements.

Economic giant

Brazil is a giant among the Latin American countries and the value of its exports and imports virtually balance. Progress is slowed only by the way the income is shared within the country and the debt owed to foreign banks.

In 2002, almost 20 per cent of the population were living below the poverty line. At times in the recent past the economy has been affected by severe inflation, and in 1992 the currency was changed from the *cruzado* to the *real* in a meticulously planned operation that brought stability and in turn helped the Brazilian image overseas. Trade grew and more and more households around the world have found Brazilian goods in their shops.

£36.9 billion
(Transport equipment, metallurgical products, soya beans, bran, oils, chemicals, iron ore, coffee)

EXPORTS

IMPORTS

£38.5 billion
(Machinery and equipment, electrical equipment, chemicals, oil, electricity)

◄◄ A comparison of the value and content of Brazil's imports and exports.

Position in South America

Brazil's independence from Portugal in September 1822 came at a time when many of the neighbouring countries were winning independence from Spain by war. Brazil declared independence and moved forward with Prince Pedro, the heir to the Portuguese throne, as the head of state. This smooth transition helped Brazil to prosper while other South American countries struggled.

Modern Brazil, with strongly nationalistic and tolerant citizens, soon came to be seen as the land of the future. The people have not changed but regional circumstances have and Brazil now faces two challenges – the rising domestic poverty and finding new markets for trade.

Images of Native Americans in Brazil, like this Yanomami Indian, have brought worldwide awareness of the destruction of the rainforests. ▼▼

⌐ DATABASE

Chronology of Historical Events 1962 to present-day

1964–1984
Military rule

1984
After the sudden death of Tancredo Neves, the president elect, vice president José Sarney takes office

1994
The 'Plan Real' of Finance Minister Fernando Henrique Cardoso successfully controls severe inflation

1995
Cardoso becomes president. During the 1990s, worldwide economic chaos affected the stability of the real

 ## Web Search ►►

► www.lanic.utexas.edu/ la.brazil/economy/
The University of Texas has a service in English known as LANIC that gives coverage of the Brazilian economy and development.

► http://www.guia-mercosur.com/
Tables and charts about the trading organization Mercosur – the member countries and its future plans.

► http://www.europa.eu. int/comm/external_ relations/mercosur/intro/ index.htm
Site highlighting the European Union's links with Mercosur.

Area:
8,511,965 square kilometres

Population size:
175,572,000

Capital city:
Brasilia (population 2.1 million including the federal district)

Other major cities:
São Paulo   (metropolitan area 18.3 million)
Rio de Janeiro (6 million)
Belo Horizonte (2.2 million)
Manaus (1.4 million)

Longest national river:
Rio São Francisco (3,161 kilometres). The River Amazon (3,158 kilometres in Brazil), is not totally Brazilian.

Highest mountain:
Pico da Neblina (3,014 metres)

Currency:
Real (plural Reis)
1 real = 100 centavos

Flag:
The flag is green with a large yellow diamond in the centre bearing a blue celestial globe with

27 white five-pointed stars. The stars represent the states of Brazil and the federal district. The globe has a white equator-like band with the motto *Ordem e Progresso* – Order and Progess. November 19 is the Day of the Flag.

Language:
Official: Portuguese
Others include Native American languages

Natural resources:
Bauxite, iron ore, manganese, nickel, phosphates, platinum, tin, uranium, petroleum, hydropower, timber

Major exports:
Agricultural products, food products, steel, motor vehicles, aircraft, machinery, timber, tin and aluminium ore, textiles, shoes, pharmaceuticals

Some national holidays and festivals:
New Year's Day (1 January)
Carnival (February or March, four days before Ash Wednesday)
21st Tiradentes Day (April)
Labour Day (1 May)
Independence Day (7 September)
Our Lady of the Aparecida (12 October)
Proclamation of the Republic (15 November)
Immaculate Conception (8 December)
Christmas Day (25 December)
Individual states may have their own additional holidays.

Official religion:
80 per cent nominally Roman Catholic. Other religions include Protestant, Buddhist, Afro-Brazilian and Native American

Glossary

AMAZONIA
That part of Brazil drained by the Amazon River.

CARNAVAL
Portuguese for 'carnival' – a pre-Lent festival celebration.

COLONIES
Countries or territories taken over or ruled by other countries.

DEMOCRATIC
Based on democracy – a form of government in which the power rests in the will of the people.

DEPUTIES (CHAMBER OF)
People appointed to act on behalf of the individual states.

ECONOMY
The basis on which a country's wealth is organized.

ENVIRONMENT
The natural world including wildlife, oceans, landscape and the atmosphere.

EXPORTS
Goods and services sold by a country to other countries.

FEDERAL (GOVERNMENT)
A form of government in which two or more states work together while maintaining some independence.

GROSS DOMESTIC PRODUCT (GDP)
The value of all the goods and services produced by a country over a year or other period.

HYDRO–ELECTRIC POWER (HEP)
Electricity generated from the energy of water movement.

IMMIGRANT
A person from one country who enters another country to live there.

IMPORTS
Goods and services bought by a country from other countries.

INDEPENDENCE
Governing of a country by its own people.

LIFE EXPECTANCY
The age to which someone may be expected to live.

MERCOSUR/MERCOSUL
A South American trading organization. The name is shortened from Spanish/Portuguese for Southern Market – currently Argentina, Uruguay, Brazil and Paraguay.

NATIVE AMERICANS
The original inhabitants of the American continents. Brazilians say *povos indigenas* – indigenous peoples.

PAULISTA/PAULISTANO
A person from the state/city of São Paulo.

REPUBLIC
An independent country whose head of state is an elected president.

SATELLITE
1) a town that is close and related to a city 2) an object in orbit round a planet.

STATE
body or unit that is responsible for its affairs. Individual states in Brazil have powers within the framework of the federal.

Index